# Off-guard

BEAUTIFUL PEOPLE UNVEILED BEFORE THE CAMERA LENS

# Ron Galella

*with an introduction by Bruce Jay Friedman*

GREENWICH HOUSE
Distributed by Crown Publishers, Inc.
New York

This 1983 edition is published by Greenwich House, a division of Arlington House, Inc., distributed by Crown Publishers, Inc., by arrangement with McGraw-Hill Book Company.

Manufactured in the United States of America

**Library of Congress Cataloging in Publication Data**

Galella, Ron.
    Offguard: Beautiful People Unveiled Before the Camera Lens

    1. Photography—Portraits.    2. Photography,
Journalistic.    I. Title.
TR681.F3G34    1983    779'.23'0924    83-5502
ISBN: 0-517-41368X

h g f e d c b a

Photo of Galella and Brando on page 92 by Peter L. Gould.
Photo of Galella in boat on page 80 by Tom Wargacki
Photo of Galella in helmet on page 94 by Paul Schmulbach
Photo of Galella with Angeleen on page 142 by Gene Spatz

# Introduction by Bruce Jay Friedman

Ron Galella first came to my attention as the result of a magazine assignment in which I was instructed to have a high old time investigating "some weird *paparazzo*" with an obsessional need to take unauthorized pictures of Jacqueline Onassis. I had no interest whatsoever in the subject but proceeded to attack it with vigor and dedication since I needed the money. I did not have a high old time. Come to think of it, I may never have had a high old time. Blocking the smooth execution of my work was the quality of Galella's photographs. Rather disturbingly, I found them to be gentle, shy, knowing, generous—every bit as lovely in their technique as their celebrated subject was in profile. This was a nuisance since—in the great tradition of magazine journalism—I had made up my mind in advance about Galella and determined that his work was to be rude and ragamuffinish. Gallantly, then, I would ride to the rescue of the fair Jacqueline and send this rude interloper back to the Cannes Film Festival, wagging his Nikon behind him. There was no way, however, that Galella's photographs could be shoved into some unlovely category. They were quietly exceptional, and I was forced to recommend (sweeping aside vast considerations of personal privacy) that Mrs. Onassis end all controversy by allowing Galella to take pictures of her unimpeded and unrestrained.

This, in retrospect, was idiotic. A Galella, allowed to go about his business, with no one on hand to rip off his fake mustache or pin his arms, is a minestrone with no salt, pepper and oregano. The very nature of his work requires that he be the uninvited guest, the man behind the potted palm, forced to swoop down on his subjects so that they could be caught offguard.

To be a *paparazzo* is to be something of a bandit. If this reckless observation has any accuracy, then America is fortunate in having as its premiere member of the breed a rather gentle mugger who forgets to frighten his victims, proceeds to reassure them and sends them away with a memorable photographic souvenir of the evening's festivities. In studying the photographs of Galella's "vic-

*top to bottom:*
Diana Rigg, Richard Burton, Duchess of Windsor, Sonny Bono, Julie Christie.

3

tims" there appears—in all but a few notorious cases—to be a conspiratorial wink, an invitation to be sweetly robbed, a need to be caught attractively offguard. The notables in question would seem to have enough size and achievement to trust the look of themselves unadorned; they ask only that the masked intruder be free of cynicism, roguishly trustworthy. Galella.

What is the nature of his art or craft or gift or whatever it is that he does so well and signs with so ever increasingly a distinctive signature? Here is Anthony Quinn, imprisoned in a tux, the civilized bandit, chafing to head up a gypsy caravan; John Huston, genially, mischievously prepared to leap into the archives of film greats; *Playboy's* Hef, all stereo and bold new life-style; Gregory Peck, yearning to be nominated as the "good" Ronnie Reagan; Cybill Shepherd, holding a quarter of herself cold, beyond reach; Jack Nicholson, quirkily listening to his own—never the studio's—drummer; Bette Davis and Joan Crawford, setting to rest the myth that lines enrich only the faces of aging men; Mick Jagger, befuddled, wondering what the next step is when you've circled the universe and you're under forty; Shelley Winters, the light and airy part of her surfacing, ironically, in the teeth of extra poundage.

Galella's pictures seem always to add to their subjects, rarely to diminish. Wrinkles become lace, great noses turn into beacons of truth, tininess is transformed into reverse height; shyness takes on a coloration of strength. No small part of his achievement is that his photographs appear—falsely, as it turns out—to be the result of long hours of arduous preparation. It is as if he has devised mysterious sittings in which there is no sitting involved. His subjects are generally on the move. More often than not he has had to leap behind a bush or a coatrack to get at them. Yet for the most part his touch is calm, his people relaxed, the beautiful and the great, staring confidently at history with Galella, the generous host, as their guide.

There is a rumor about that Galella now speaks openly of art and respectability. This is an atrocious turn of events. Let the powers that be immediately combine to block this development. All possible obstacles must be thrown in his path, no effort spared to keep him hounded, harassed, in a constant state of torment. Only in this hellish manner can the man be expected to flourish, to refine further his rough photographic magic, to add to his raffishly impressive body of work.

# A Paparazzo View by Ron Galella

We want heroes—and when we don't get them, we create them. I suppose this is because we need heroes—picture stories we can follow with the eye, the heart tagging along behind—so that the eye first and then the heart are thus distracted from every kind of bad and worsening news and the cruel tedium of our unheroic lives. There's no sin in wanting to escape. I sometimes think that our enduring and limitless capacity to escape from the realities that dog us is the gift the angels give us. In any case, heroes—nowadays we call them "celebrities" or "stars"—are here to stay. And I for one am glad of it. Because my passion is to show the world the stars it celebrates in the natural and spontaneous moods that only *paparazzo* photo-journalism can capture. I'm not interested in the packaged image, the sort of posed, retouched glossy favored by the official and unofficial corps of press agents who in one way or another service the celebrity industry. What I am interested in conveying to a public that wants it is the nonplasticized core of the people who fire the excitement and fascination of so many of us. I am interested in printing onto film what is real. And as this book hopes to make clear, pursuing what is real in a world of packaged fame is no easy job. It is a job thick with risks, threats, occasional violence and sometimes the necessary folly that courts humiliation and ridicule. But I don't care. I see myself as the dean of American *paparazzo* photo-journalism—a self-appointed role, perhaps, but one I figure I've paid the dues to own. I love my work—and I'm good at it. Maybe the best at it.

But don't misunderstand. My aim is not to strip the celebrity of glamour by catching him unaware. On the contrary, I want to reveal the real glamour that I believe is natural to every celebrity— the *essence* that helped to make him a celebrity in the first place and that's often masked once stardom is achieved. And that's why I *must* catch my subjects offguard, without preparation. To catch the light to what's underneath.

My style of photographing celebrities is called the *paparazzo* approach because that's pretty much what it is. *Paparazzo* is the Italian term usually used for a free-floating, freelance photographer—and it owes to the distinguished Italian film director Federico

*top to bottom:*
Evel Knievel, Martha Mitchell, Bette Davis, Fred Astaire, Julie Andrews.

5

Fellini. While creating *La Dolce Vita*, Fellini assigned the name "Signor Paparazzo" to a character in the film, a photographer who was always scurrying up and down Rome's Via Veneto snapping candids of movie stars and other strolling celebrities.

What we're talking about, then, is completely unrehearsed photography, where the expression and gesture are thoroughly spontaneous and unique to the moment and circumstance. You have to go after people *where* and *when* you *can*, discover them in natural situations, without appointments, without an alert of any kind. And, as I said, that's not easy. Since almost all photographers shooting for major publications work by appointment through a crew of protective front men, the celebrity can control his image, have the publicity he needs and wants but have it on his *own* terms. The results are lifeless, canned; certainly the pictures that come out of routine photo sessions dare show nothing that would surprise or reveal. Famous personalities retain press agents for the sole purpose of widening a reputation but only in ways that are in keeping with the pre-fab image the personality wishes presented to the public. What results is not information but propaganda, not news but advertising.

But I believe that I am a *news* photographer and that it is only proper for me, like other journalists, to use my reporting materials as I choose and as I think best serves newsgathering. The only difference is that I don't use a pad and pencil. I use a camera—and I use it justly. For me, this is the only game, the only celebrity-reporting that matters. But the only game is a hard game. Breaking through the wall of press agents and bodyguards to get directly to the stars, tracking them down and photographing them in airports, streets, theaters, hotel lobbies and other public places calls for some tough times. Sometimes I get what I want, the *real* story. But sometimes I get a lawsuit—or a sock in the jaw.

A freelancer who works for the "story" as I do must gamble energy, time and out-of-pocket expenses to produce pictures on pure speculation. He's investing against all odds. Of course he hopes it will pay off with that special photograph, a new look at someone the world has many times seen the old way, a look *into* someone, into perhaps what makes that person so adored, so admired. I don't think you have to be Italian to be a good *paparazzo*, but you do have to have plenty of drive and determination. And a little old-fashioned American pluck doesn't hurt any, either.

I recognize the fundamental but opposing rights involved in the question of *paparazzo* photo-journalism. On the one hand, you must respect a person's right to privacy. On the other hand, the

public has the right to be informed. So be it. But public figures who in all ways show that they seek recognition *surrender* the right of privacy. And certainly they must give up that right when they show themselves in public places (or even when they can readily be observed *from* public places). This was the position the court took in the much discussed 1972 debate between myself and Jacqueline Kennedy Onassis. Whereas Jackie argued that she was a public figure only during the time she spent in the White House and that she thereafter was a housewife and mother with a right to privacy in public places, the court decided *once a celebrity, always a celebrity.* The court upheld me in the argument that Jacqueline Kennedy Onassis is a public figure whose right to privacy in public places must be waived in favor of the public's right to be informed—and in so ruling the court held to a position on support of freedom of the press. I think the 1972 decision was a vitally important one—for *all* journalists, whether they report by word or by photograph.

Yet the risks of the *paparazzo*'s art are no less great since the 1972 decision—long stake-outs and often nothing to show for it, heavy expenses that are not underwritten by magazine or newspaper assignment, and now and then *wham.* As everyone knows by now, I was punched in the jaw by Marlon Brando (he can *hit*), was almost killed chasing Julie Christie along the Pacific Highway, not to mention my being beaten up by Richard Burton's bodyguards in Cuernavaca and hosed down by friends of Brigitte Bardot (don't kid yourself, that can *hurt*) when I went after her with my camera on the coast of France.

Sometimes I think *every* celebrity in the whole wide world is passing the instructions that Jackie shouted to a Secret Service man one day when I was trying to take some pictures of her: "Smash his camera!"

Okay, *smash* my camera. I'll get another one. Because practicing my trade is my right, my duty and my sole ambition in this life. And the more I work at this risky game, the more I am convinced it is the only game for the true photo-journalist, for the picture-reporter who is in unafraid pursuit of the truest picture.

This book records the truest pictures of hundreds of celebrities, many of whom are *my* heroes, too. Well, of course, they are: I picked them. I admire and even love many of these people. I don't want to show them up. I just want to show them—in a light that shines on the distinct feature that made them great: the unique feeling, energy and grandeur that is fundamentally and richly in them.

*top to bottom:*
Ben Vereen, Joanne Woodward, Valerie Perrine, Al Pacino, Barbra Streisand.

Robert Redford researching the gait of reporter Robert Woodward. Redford plays Woodward in the film version of All the President's Men, *the best-selling Woodward and Carl Bernstein book about the unfolding of the Watergate break-in story.*

The Redfords on a bus. You get the feeling that Bob would leap to give up his seat to a lady—and you're right. He would.

The Redfords showing up for Barefoot in the Park premiere. They both had less hair in those days. They weren't so easy to spot, but they were a lot more visible.

# Robert Redford

Every once in a while the screen produces a star who typifies the American ideal, a dead-center sense of ourselves in keeping with the spirit of the time. Such a star was Gary Cooper in his day—slow, tall, weathered, a man who suggested boulders. The mid-Seventies gives us Robert Redford whether we like it or not (and generally we do), a fellow we can quickly identify as the boy next door, a *familiar* model, yet a man who suggests to us that he's looked into the dark places, that he's seen enough to be beyond surprise. I guess the feeling you have is that the Coop could rescue your house from bad guys but Bob could save it from bad vibes. Like the Newmans, the Redfords are solid family people, people in touch with the enduring things in life. I think it's his connection with the *home* and with the Idaho country of his wife's birth that gives Bob his special grace and his increasing appeal. As meticulus with his dress as with his choice of roles, he knows what's really Redford. He turned down *The Graduate, Midnight Cowboy,* and *Who's Afraid of Virginia Woolf* because they weren't right for him. He's a natural star; the man you see on the screen is the same man you catch strolling down Fifth Avenue. Anyhow, he's great to photograph—because he always looks like Redford and he always looks great no matter how you shoot him.

*The Redfords and their children out for a Sunday stroll. Let aspiring* paparazzi *and old-fashioned rubberneckers note: Yesterday—Hollywood and Vine. Today it's 59th and Fifth.*

*After one day's work on* Three Days of the Condor.

*Bob's smiling—but that's because he's got the guard there to shield him from the usual photographers. But yours truly, shooting from under the elbow, got the pic.*

*Redford looking clean, tousled and all-American during a break on the set of* Three Days of the Condor.

11

*Dynamic Dancing Duo—Wetson (Errol) and Hemingway (Margaux). He's famous for hamburgers. She's famous for being related. He doesn't cook. She doesn't write. But what does it matter? They're famous, anyway—which is a full-time and, as you can see, exhausting occupation.*

*Margaux Hemingway.*

*Margaux Hemingway and Joe Namath at press party to promote Fabergé's new fragrance, "Babe." Joe seems to favor the plastic babe over the real one.*

*Rudolf Nureyev.* *They haven't choreographed the dance Rudi can't do—or the woman who won't do it with him.*

*Rudi with Everybody's Friend Monique Van Vooren.*

*You may not recognize the face, but you can bet Ivory Snow will never forget the rest of her. That's Marilyn Chambers; her partner is playboy Huntington Hartford.*

*Linda Lovelace of Deep Throat fame. What's she doing—warming-up exercises?*

14

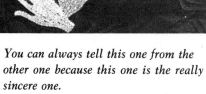

*You can always tell this one from the other one because this one is the really sincere one.*

*Zsa Zsa, Eva and Mother Jolie Gabor—available for weddings, wakes, bar-mitzvahs and dog fights.*

Rock-world titans John Lennon and David Bowie in
their Sunday-go-to-meetin' best.

Ex-Beatle John Lennon and wife Yoko
Ono in a public exhibition of private
feelings.

16

*Britt Eklund with boy friend rock star Rod Stewart.*

Rock star Mick Jagger. The wages of fame are not all bankable.

Bianca Jagger, looking as if she's seen it all. Chances are she has.

*Grand Old Man of Pop, Andy Warhol. His age makes it easier to take him seriously. Too bad he had to wait so long for us to catch up.*

19

*Some très, très fashionable people including*
*très, très actor Sal Mineo; and plain old transvestite*
*Candy Darling at an After Dark soiree.*

*Two Italian works of art: Michelangelo's David and Gina Lollobrigida.*

*"Pardon me, but I couldn't help noticing that perfectly
darling little jugular vein of yours."*
*William F. Buckley.*

*Norman Mailer, writer and author of* Marilyn.

*Arthur Miller, playwright and husband of Marilyn.*

*Barbara Walters and Walter Cronkite: "You say you'll make me a star?"*

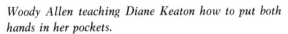

*Woody Allen teaching Diane Keaton how to put both hands in her pockets.*

*An exceptionally difficult maneuver called "The Malaysian Standing Crossover." Is he a good teacher or is she a fast learner?*

*Now here's how you do it with one hand.*

*Jack Nicholson's done just about everything in movies—scripted, directed and turned in some of the best performances in film history. And he gave me one of the truest smiles on record.*

25

*Many actors, behind their casual exteriors, are truly competitive, some more so than others.*

*It's a pleasure to come across Beautiful People who really are beautiful people. Former "Mama" turned actress Michelle Phillips and actor Jack Nicholson look as though America was never healthier.*

*Actor Warren Beatty. Not since Samson has any man done so much for hair.*

*Beatty outbeautied by Michelle Phillips and her daughter China. Mama Michelle used to be a singing "Mama."*

*Leigh Taylor-Young photographed in London.*

*It took a telephoto lens to snag a bearded Ryan O'Neal and ex-wife Leigh Taylor-Young on Malibu Beach. Malibu's a good place to hunt if you don't mind sand in your shoes.*

Here's Ryan and Academy Award–winning daughter Tatum at the Century Plaza in L.A. A father weeps, a child comforts—and the stardom they both possess is no help at all.

Tatum with a bob, a bow tie and an Oscar. The whiskery buss is courtesy of her granddad.

*The mystery man is Faye Dunaway's hubby, Peter Wolf.*

*They all imitate Bette Davis. But whatever they do,*
*it's still an imitation.*

31

*I always thought that Lillian Gish was shorter and that Helen Hayes was taller. Anyway, they're both giants.*

*Gone with the snows of yesteryear, the George Raft snarl that quickened our hearts. In its place, an old man illuminated in the soft light of fame fallen away gracefully.*

*Joey Bishop and Jack Benny: "For an encore, we're going to sneeze in harmony."*

33

*Joan Crawford and the Duke. You want a lesson in how to survive and hang on to your dignity? Here's two that could teach you the whole bit.*

*The chairman of the board of Pepsi-Cola—but to a generation of Americans she'll always be the hoofer who made it big: Joan Crawford.*

*You call him Mister Cagney—and mean it. Class tells. All Jimmy needs to do is whisper.*

*You would know this was Jimmy's daughter anywhere. As for Mrs. Cagney, doesn't she look a little, little bit like a recent First Lady?*

*Feisty Jimmy and Feisty Frank at a testimonial for Cagney. Makes you want to swing into a chorus of "Yankee Doodle Dandy" or "Young at Heart."*

Funny combination: Frank, Dinah Shore and George Plimpton? Well, why not!

Frank Sinatra: "Don't try to make a monkey outa me, friend." I didn't. I just took a shot of Frank hitching up his trousers.

Old Blue Eyes and girl friend Barbara Marx. Wonder if he called her a "broad" to her face or behind her back?

# Frank Sinatra

I can't think of any star who has held the status of superstar as long as Frank Sinatra has—and the man did it *twice*, returning from the days when he was worshiped by the bobby-sox and rocking-chair sets, like no singer *ever*, to even *greater* adoration in the Sixties and Seventies— and now it seems that no matter what Sinatra does, his fame will go on increasing. He could probably beat up old ladies and get cheers for it—and a bigger recording contract. There is no question that a lot of Frank's appeal stems from his alleged underworld connections and from his hobnobbing with the nobs and the politicos. It seems everybody wants to be in Frankie's company no matter what his manners are like—and I think this is because Sinatra suggests something beyond simple celebrity. I think this something has to do with Frank's tough-guy/nice-guy coloring and our never knowing which hue of Frank is going to show up. The guy can surprise you, really dump you on your ear, and we like that. We *like* knowing Frank might curtsy to the Queen of England and then, rising, snort, "How ya doin', toots? Gettin' any?" It's this quality in Sinatra that makes him the perfect American hero—the scruffy, scrappy kid with ravioli in his pockets who rises to international eminence just because he wanted to and you couldn't stop him—and who is still snickering at the swells who are going nuts to rub up against him. I guess we've elevated Frank Sinatra to the top of the superstar heap because he, above all, embodies the American Dream made good, the democratic ideal in all its readily understood sentimentality.

*Frank sporting whiskers for an upcoming movie role.*

*Sinatra and his family at his father's interment in New Jersey.*

*At the Senate Crime Committee hearing in Washington, D.C. The heavy is big Jilly Rizzo, bodyguard and close friend.*

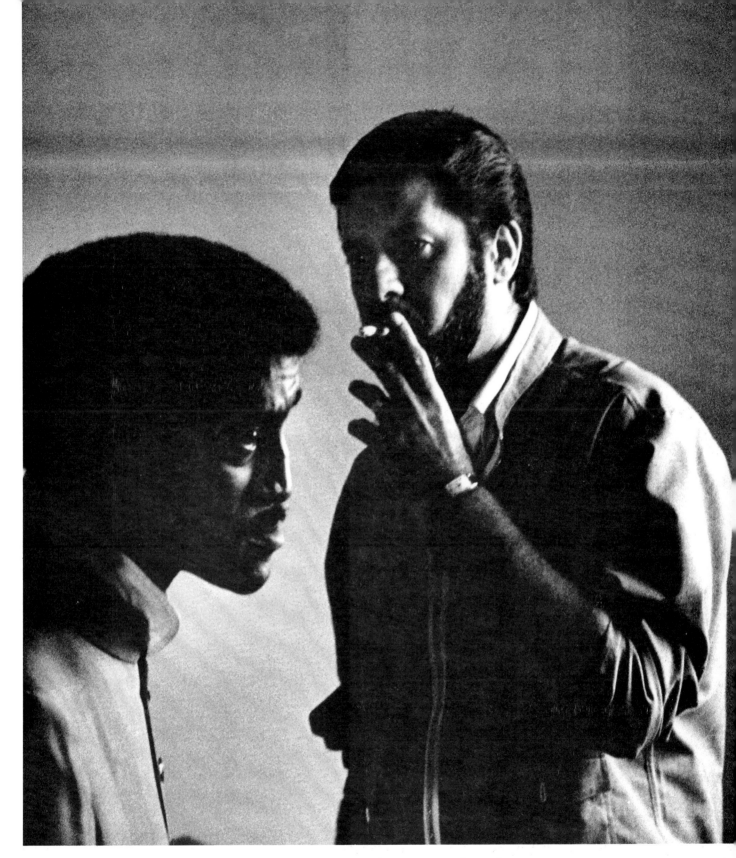

*Sammy Davis, Jr., and Jerry Lewis.*

*Maybe Dean was gagging it up—maybe he wasn't. Either way, he's using his lapel to hide the hootch from ex-wife Jeannie and—you guessed it—Cardinal Spellman.*

*Dean looks as if he's just seen the moon hit the sky like a big pizza pie. He just saw me is all.*

*Now here's where Dino did see the moon hit the sky like a big pizza pie.*

*The eye has it.*

*Raquel Welch and All in the Family Carroll O'Connor making like Little Orphan Annie and Daddy Warbucks. Just watch your hands, old man.*

*Come to think of it, her legs ain't so bad, either.*

*Raquel Welch at a fashion show. Whoever he is, baby, he's not for you.*

*Ali just out of her mind over singer Andy Williams. (He's telling her she looks gorgeous in butter lettuce, but has she ever considered wearing a rutabaga?)*

*Ali so mad for James Caan she could just die! (He told her where she could pick up some spinach wholesale.)*

*Steve McQueen: For crying out loud, Ali, they're laughing. I told you not to wear an artichoke in your ear tonight! Ali: And I told you, dumb nose, Bergdorf's was all out of turnips.*

*Ali just craaazzy for ex-husband Evans. (Hey, you can see where Bergdorf's got in a shipment of escarole!)*

"Bob said if I could get this off the table and past the doorman, I could wear it tomorrow night."

*Ali accompanied by Ryan O'Neal catches sight of a vegetable vendor in L.A.*

*Paul and his daughter Nell. Proud dad? Or proud daughter? I'd say both.*

*Paul and gifted actress wife Joanne Woodward. Their marriage has made it through the rough times.*

# Paul Newman

I see Paul Newman as representing something very different from Robert Redford, the handiest comparison. Both men have classic American "good looks," but you would never let Paul into your heart as the boy next door. Paul would work his way into your heart, all right, but only as the mysterious world traveler visiting town after twenty years' absence touring exotic ports as a merchant seaman. Paul is hard-edged—right down to the squared, bony cut of his face. Yet he's very much the family man—concerned about his home, his wife, his children and the life of the mind. There's nothing Hollywood about Paul, nor is there any tinsel in his extraordinarily gifted wife, Joanne Woodward. You've got to admit the Newmans are engaged in their work and in each other, and you can't help liking and admiring them for it. And though they certainly don't welcome being photographed by other than a movie camera, neither Paul nor Joanne would lose his cool and give the *paparazzi* a hard time. They're not the rumpus-raising kind, unless it's about something that matters to them—and matters to other grownups: the nation's political fortunes, the making of a good piece of acting or entertainment. The Newmans know who they are and are so consistently what they are that no camera could tell a different story.

*Paul at a McGovern rally.*

*Paul's a solid family man. I got him here at a birthday party for Eli Wallach, calling home to see if the kids were all right.*

*Joanne Woodward and Mrs. Paul Newman—a woman of dimension and an actress of true stature.*

Donald Sutherland.

*Karen Black thrilled to pieces by her New York Film
Critics Award.*

*McQueen has a wonderfully rugged and very human face—a face that we would like yet find unnotable, unless of course we knew he was a star. (But even he sometimes forgets.)*

53

*The one and only Dorothy Lamour: Remember all those* On the Road to . . . *movies she made? Well, take a look at the glorious countenance of the well-seasoned traveler.*

*You can't have Hope and Lamour in your collection without adding Der Bingle. So here's Crosby with familiar props: wife Kathryn and pipe.*

Hope: I beg your pardon, Miss, but I couldn't help noticing we have something unusual in common. I'll bet you're wearing a Goodyear 48 with a double-D cup.
Gleason: No, as a matter of fact I'm wearing a Lockheed strapless with reinforced elastic by American Machine and Foundry.

*Bob "Eat Your Heart Out, Twiggy" Hope—at Honor America Day in D.C.*

**Here's a man who occupies** space, *not because he's big around his middle but because he's big around the heart. Jackie Gleason, we love you, Mr. Big Guy.*

55

*This took some doing. You can see the bushes up against my lens. Hell, you don't catch Doris Day swimming with a dog in her own backyard, unless you know when and where to wait and how fast to run when the dogs start barking at you.*

*When Doris found out about these shots, she had a ten-foot wall built around her pool. I don't blame her a bit.*

*This is the one that really burned her up. If you ask me, at her age she should be proud.*

*But I like Doris. How could you not like a sweetheart with a face like this?*

*Ann Miller cutting up. Ah, those guys in the chorus line have all the fun.*

*Ava Gardner at Chasen's. Va-va varoom!*

*Jane Russell at Roseland. Hey, come on, Jane—show us what you got famous for in* The Outlaw. *That's right—your teeth!*

*Debbie Reynolds telling Truman Capote that he's the greatest writer who ever lived and Truman Capote telling Debbie Reynolds she's right.*

*Debbie Reynolds and daughter Carrie Fisher. A kiss or a kiss-off?*

*Don't worry if you know the face but just can't place this guy. He always wears an* Open End *T-shirt. Also matching jockey shorts. His name's David Susskind.*

*Hank and the latest Mrs. Fonda, Shirlee. Oh well, underneath all the glitter and the tinsel they're just like you and me, right?*

*Actor Lee J. Cobb at Sardi's. He made Willie Loman a nationally tragic figure—and Willie Loman made him a nationally respected artist.*

*An original looking at an original—Zero Mostel in front of his own painting at his gallery opening.*

The divine Judy Garland in her triumphant return to the Palace Theater.

It was at 63rd and York Avenue that I found gold in the rainy New York streets—Garbo the magnificent.

I snapped Judy at El Morocco the night she opened at the Palace, and zing went the strings of my heart.

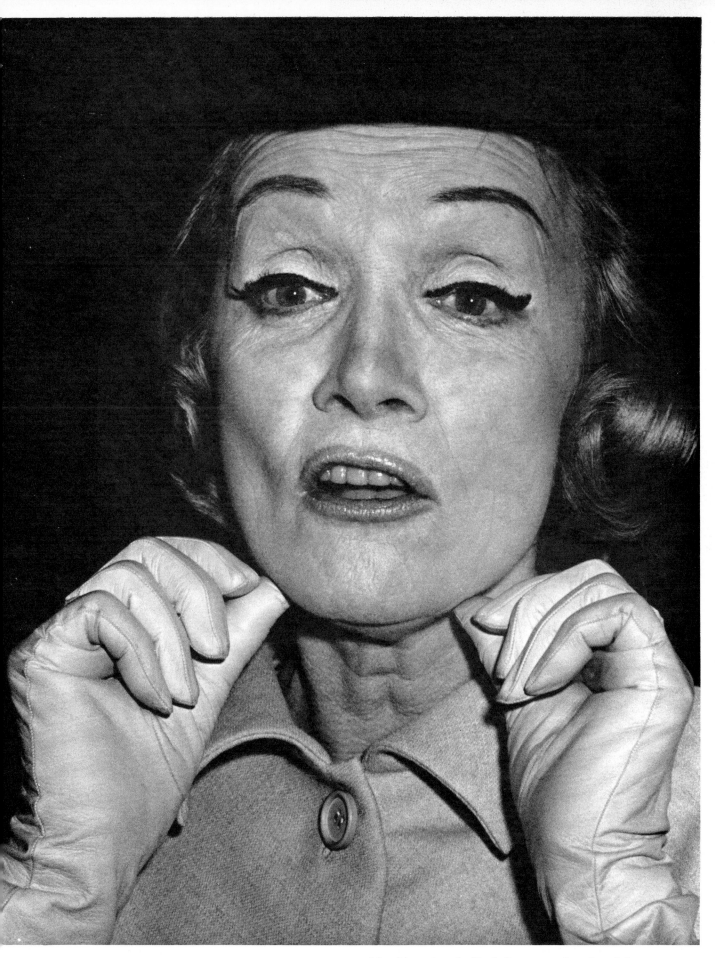

*No, this isn't a double Italian curse that slipped, but the enduring Marlene Dietrich aiming her face.*

*Liza Minnelli: "I used to smoke asparagus, but it made me bite my fingernails."*

*Liza with dad Vincente Minnelli being welcomed to Rainbow Room party in her honor. They love you, Liza.*

*Judy's daughter Liza Minnelli. You look at those eyes and you see the big hunger that carried her all the way to the top.*

*An early shot of Liza.*

*Liza and half-sister Lorna Luft. Come on, Liza honey, they really love you. Sure they do.*

*From Funny Girl to Funny Lady.*

Here's Barbra with friend Jon Peters.

Streisand with star-gazing half-sister Roz Kind, who's made a few bucks styling her songs like Barbra's. But that's okay. It's all in the family.

Barbra Streisand: Who else? Bunny-rabbit earmuffs are a swell disguise, but it's not the ears that give you away, Barbra.

*In a way, I think this shot of Presley proves my point—the deep private thing he's holding inside him, the thing the public never sees—except maybe a glimpse now and then.*

# Elvis Presley

Elvis is easily the most highly protected of the superstars, and I find him even more enigmatic than Sinatra. The man is puzzling, a whirlpool of contradictions. But what surfaces is the face of a rough boy spoiling for a fight. And yet the man's manner is soft, almost purring—and which of us will ever forget the incredibly gentle delivery he gives to the song "Love Me Tender"? But the curl of his lip, the barely concealed contempt, the flash of his dress and the hasty thrust of his body all suggest a man staggering around in something close to a dangerous social and sexual rage. But of course it's the opposing quality of little-boy-lost that sets the whole Presley dynamic in motion. It was the same combination that made James Dean a national hero in the space of just three movies—and it's a combination that has made Presley one of the biggest money-makers in show-business history and has kept him fabulously popular long after the novelty of his raucous song-styling and suggestive gyrations wore off. It would be great to hear Elvis explain himself, but he's not talking. He's a great mystery. It would be wonderful to photograph the nucleus of his secret story. But Elvis is too well guarded for me to catch him utterly offguard. So I've had to draw a photographic portrait of him by taking pictures around the perimeter of the inner man. They come, I think, as close as anything visual *could* come to telling the truth about this curious man and enduring superstar.

*A quick sip between songs.*

*There's a guy named Jim Curtain who dresses up like Elvis and follows him around as a decoy. Sometimes he even fools us paparazzi. Here's Curtain signing an autograph.*

*Elvis and his fifteen bodyguards leave the Philadelphia Hilton through the kitchen exit. Presley probably has better security than the President of the United States—at least a dozen bodyguards whenever he goes public. The only guy more untouchable than Elvis is Howard Hughes. Believe me—I know.*

Elvis's ex-wife Priscilla wearing a gown she designed. I took this shot in the Presley home, which Priscilla is proud to tell you she decorated.

The eighteen-room Memphis mansion Elvis lives in. Weird, the stately house in the background and the flashy gate in the foreground. Who knows—maybe the two things tell us something secret about Elvis—what he shows and what he doesn't show.

*The Great Cinema Director Federico Fellini. I revere this great artist. He coined the term that now names my style of photography—and sometimes I think he invented films.*

*Here's one of my all-time favorite faces. Anna Magnani's got the look of a woman who makes you think of bread baking and passion rising.*

French film star Jean-Paul Belmondo on the set. Conventional good looks don't matter to a French audience as much as they do here. But that's changing now—and Belmondo's American popularity has helped the healthy trend.

*Right after the premiere of Dr. Zhivago, I asked Sophia Loren what she liked best about the picture's star, Omar Shariff. "His eyes," Sophia answered, demonstrating with her immensely expressive hands.*

*Beautiful and expressive on the David Frost Show.*

*An affectionate glance at husband Carlo Ponti.*

# Sophia Loren

Is it possible that this exquisitely endowed, marvelously talented, breath-takingly beautiful woman is actually middle-aged? And is married to the same man—producer Carlo Ponti—for over a quarter century? That she prepares her own meals, makes her own bed, even washes her own lingerie? And is resolutely devoted to her sons, Eli and Cipi? Is this a rampant display of media hype? The latest P.R. drivel from a salaried studio flack? My own research suggests she is extraordinary—and more: a female Horatio Alger story of success, with the depth and character to make it count. Born out of wedlock in a Rome charity hospital, raised by grandparents in the grinding poverty of wartorn Italy, discovered at age fifteen in a Rome beauty contest by Carlo Ponti, twenty-one years her senior, and ending up as one of the world's wealthiest, most beautiful, and—yes—happiest actresses. Sophia and Carlo's home is a fifty-room, sixteenth-century palace in the Roman hills, although most of their time in recent years is spent in their Paris penthouse, with rest stops in their apartments in New York and Geneva, a farm in Tuscany, and a chalet in the French Alps. We could envy—even hate—a dozen other celebrities for that good fortune, but Sophia—cheers, we love you.

*Lips and eyes to set you dreaming—and the promise of
a soul inside to make it a dream of paradise.*

*"Of course it's your intelligence I admire most of all."*

*Sophia and son, "Cipi" (Carlo, Jr.), head for Rome.*

*Sophia and family.*

*Dick said, "You've had enough. One more shot and . . ." Liz had to keep him from slugging me. You can see how angry Dick is from the way he's holding his body.*

*Here's where I caught Liz and Dick switching planes at Kennedy Airport. The shot shows something vibrant in Burton, something correspondingly submissive in Taylor.*

*Robert Kennedy, Liz, Dick and Ethel Kennedy—the first pictures I took of Liz and Dick. There was a party at the Plaza Hotel, no photographers invited, which was good news because most photographers give up when they're told to stay out. But I don't give up. I got into a tuxedo, put my cameras under my jacket and sneaked up onto a balcony overlooking the ballroom.*

# Burton & Taylor

It is only in combination that Burton and Taylor are the greatest superstars. Or, to say it exactly the way I mean it, there's only *one* superstar here and that's Burton/Taylor, Liz/Dick. Oh sure, each achieved fame in his own right (although Liz probably ultimately outshines Burton), but neither enjoyed anything like the attention he now has as part of a team. Well, team isn't the way to put it. Burton and Taylor aren't so much a team as they are a public squabble, a long-running family scrap appearing on tour for an elite international audience in all the world's exotic ports. Ultimately, their private lives are of greater interest than their careers.

The Liz/Dick appeal is pretty much like the thing a really good soap opera has going for it—and with the earlier marriages, intervening romances, and comet-tail of children that spin off from the red-hot center, there's always material for a new chapter to pep up failing public interest. Right now, in fact, there's probably no other continuing saga that so excites our attention. Liz/Dick have proved themselves endlessly inventive at keeping us on the edge of our seats waiting for the next crisis, the next irony, the next heart-warming kiss-kiss and reconciliation.

I took this time exposure of myself staked out across from the Kalizma. See the sacks of sugar and coffee beans? They were my bed for the weekend. And that window was my TV.

One of the worst stake-outs to get pictures was when I holed up for the weekend in a rat-filled warehouse on the Thames where the Burtons' yacht the Kalizma was moored. The Burtons had brought their dogs to London with them, but the English health authorities wouldn't let them bring the dogs into the city, so Liz and Dick had to leave them on the yacht and visit them on board during the weekends. There was no bathroom, but the worst thing was the rats. I'll go through hell for pictures—and that's just what I had to do to go after the Burtons on the Kalizma.

All that work, and this is what I got—Liz and one of the mates putting up a screen to shield the stern from rubberneckers and some Kalizma crewmen watching a boat race.

Liz and Dick leaving the Queen Elizabeth at Le Havre. Shortly after this shot, Dick said to me: "If you intend to follow me to the south of France, I shall have to be constrained from killing you."

When I went after Dick and Liz on the coast of France, I tried the old-sailor-disguise routine that worked for Jackie on Skorpios. Nothing more natural than a picture-taking sailor.

*At the Plaza I called out "Richard!" to get his attention, and what I got was this hostile look. Yeah, I cooled it after this shot.*

*Liz at Land's End greeting a polio victim who accepted her donation for polio research.*

*Here's Taylor—in total detail.*

*Dancin' in the dark:*
*Lauren Bacall and Yul Brynner.*

*David Niven and Rock Hudson breaking for coffee*
*during a rehearsal. It's rare one catches stars looking*
*as if they don't know their next line.*

I had to pose as a mailman to snag
these photos of Brigitte Bardot at St.
Tropez.

Some actors are an actor's actor, just as some men are a man's man. Walter Matthau—we may all be pleased at our good fortune—is both.

Matthau on his way to a baseball game? Fencing some swiped goods? Seeing which is heavier, the clothes bag or the radio? All of the above or none of the above?

*Impish Jack and the gamin Mrs. Lemmon beating a retreat from the Plaza after the rascal's fiftieth birthday party.*

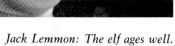

*Jack Lemmon: The elf ages well.*

85

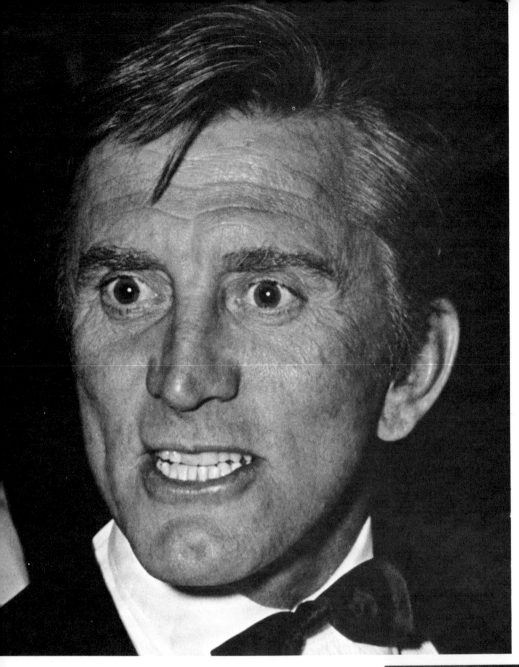

Sometimes a star's expressions offscreen are telling:
you figure either this person is always *acting* or he's
never acting. As for Kirk Douglas, snapped here at
Sardi's, I'd say he's on *all the time.*

Douglas climbing the stairs at the Beverly Hilton and
looking a little bit stagy offstage. Hey, ma, look—no
hands!

*Shelley gives a big hello.*

*Everybody loves old rough-'em-up, bust-'em-up Shelley Winters, waving to fans outside ABC studio.*

*Cary Grant looking like a million bucks and change as he clowns it up here with actress Helen Ross who's holding a Best Supporting Actress award that she just won for her role in* The Effects of Gamma Rays on Man in the Moon Marigolds. *See Cary's pocket flap folded under? If he was shot that way in the good old days, forty thousand guys would be doing the same number in a week.*

*And speaking of loot, notice the bill rolled in Cary's hand as he waits for a taxi. Cab fare or tip for the hotel doorman?*

*If Kate Hepburn's not the First Lady of American film, I say we all get together and demand a recount.*

*Here's what class looks like when it's just standing still and thinking. Rex Harrison.*

*Johnny and Joanna at American Film Institute Tribute to Orson Welles. You can see where Johnny's eyes are set a little close together, but you can see where Joanna's eyes fit her just right.*

*You can almost hear Johnny saying, "So who's the clown with the camera? If it's Ron Galella, call in the B-52s."*

*The only star with a more rascally face than Jack Lemmon's—Tonight show host Johnny Carson and wife Joanna.*

I got this one of Dick Cavett out at secluded Montauk on his way to mount a horse. He's wearing the dark glasses to make sure the horse knows he's a celebrity.

*Cavett bussing Gina Lollobrigida.*

Here's Cavett wearing a neckerchief and standing behind a sign with his name on it. The neckerchief is to show you he's a celebrity and the sign is to tell you which one.

*I could afford to smile like this till he broke my jaw.*

*I got this picture of Brando at New York's Apollo Theater. It suggests the man's limitless mystery and immense personal and artistic power. Certainly he is the most powerful of all American actors.*

# Marlon Brando

When it comes to disdain for the public, no star outstrips Brando. Marlon despises efforts to publicize anything about him except what Marlon wants publicized. And we all know that Marlon's been working hard for a fair deal for the Indians. Oh, Marlon's made sure we all know *that*. But how about a fair deal for everybody, Marlon—including a guy who's plying his trade with a camera and, if you'll pardon the immodesty, doing it in the maverick way you yourself have championed, in your movie roles and in real life? Well, as everybody also knows, Marlon Brando laid a good one into me with a right cross that did a lot of damage and cost him forty grand—all because Marlon Brando wants to be left alone. Well, if this great artist—perhaps the greatest American actor of all time—sincerely wants to be left alone, how come he makes his living exhibiting himself? Nobody forces him. Money he's got, and if it's work he's so crazy about, they tell me there's a shortage of good honest locksmiths. No, you'll never convince me he doesn't love being adored and sought after by millions of people he never met and will never know. Yet in an interview Marlon has said that he doesn't want to share his personal feelings with thousands of people he does not know and will never meet. That's nice. But is it legit—is it fair—if your business happens to be persuading millions of people to *adore* you and *care* about you and wonder about your personal feelings? I say a man like that has *no right* to despise folks for what he himself inspired in them. To despise them for what he has encouraged in them (and made a fortune from) is downright unjust and mean-spirited. And also immature. Anyhow, I can forgive Brando anything, even a pretty hefty belt in the mouth because no matter how much he sneers at me for the low-rent work I do, I'll never stop admiring him for the great work he does. Hell, I'd even forgive him his acting in *Desirée.*

*Here's the first picture I took of Brando. You can see the winning smile that might have inspired his folks to call him "Bud."*

*Brando stalked by our hero.*

*I shot these two pictures of Brando before he taped the Cavett show. He's seen arriving at the 60th Street heliport with two aides—and then getting ready to depart for the ABC studio by car. I guess I'll never forget the outfit he was wearing—and, now that I look at these photos, what seems the brutal weight and bulk of this strange, mysterious man and actor.*

*Here's how it happened, the famous punch Brando threw into me, the one that broke my jaw. After the Cavett taping, I followed Marlon and Dick to Chinatown. After I'd shot about a dozen pictures, Brando waved me over. He said, "What else do you want that you don't already have?" And I asked him if he could please remove his sunglasses. Then—wham! It was a surprise attack and a tremendous blow. If you've seen Marlon throw a punch in the movies—in, say,* On the Waterfront—*you know the man knows what the hell he's doing. Few stars could throw more punches that looked as if they meant it and knew what they were doing. In fact, Brando trained to fight on Broadway, and that's how he broke his nose and acquired his rough waterfront face. Take my word for it, Brando can hit like a pro.*

*"I heard hems are lower this year," whispers Bob Hope to Rocky Marciano.*

*The champ! The Manassa Mauler! Jack Dempsey himself! I don't think Jack was all that happy to see me.*

*Speaking of champs, here they are! Muhammad Ali and Joe Louis! The bigger they are, the bigger they are—and that's the whole story.*

*Every once in a while you get a lucky shot that comes up looking like the paparazzo's dream: a picture that goes right down to the hearts of the people who are in it. Here's prizefighter Jerry Quarry with his wife after Quarry was whipped by Joe Frazier.*

*Danny Kaye at a tribute to Joe DiMaggio. Well, at least he's got the mitt on the right hand. I mean, the left hand.*

*Gridiron champ Joe Namath goofballing with entertainer Ann-Margret. You're gorgeous, Joe.*

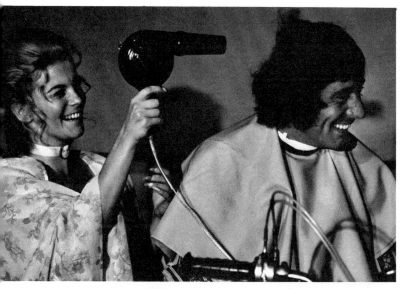

*He used to tear the field up for the Cleveland Browns; now he just tears the screen up. Jim Brown. Frankly, I don't think I would have taken this picture if the man had said no. At least I hope I wouldn't have.*

*Namath with international soccer star Pelé, the highest-paid athlete in the world.*

*"Phyllis, please, a little dignity and composure!" reprimands Bobby Riggs.*

*"Ow, Bobby, one glance at your great hairy chest and I'm melting," pleads Phyllis Diller.*

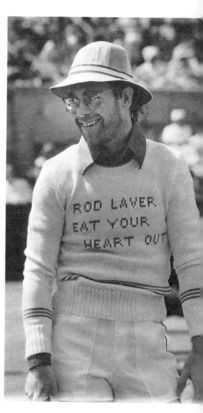

*Elton John and tennis star Billie Jean King, scourge of male-chauvinist-has-been-upstart-smart-alecks and other racket-handlers.*

*Rock star Elton John at the RFK pro-celebrity tennis tourney at Forest Hills. So who's this Rod Laver, a bass guitarist?*

You theenk to fool Ron, eh? Just get a shot of Big Burt on the 100 Rifles set.

Catch the self-conscious cuffwork. Burt Reynolds never forgets he's Burt Reynolds.

Comedienne Kaye Ballard doing her nightclub routine with a picture of . . . of . . . oh, yeah—Soupy Sales? (Just kiddin', Burt. We'd know your belly button anywhere.)

*Shirley MacLaine and Pete Hamill at a party for Art Buchwald thrown by Irv Lazar at the Bistro. How's that for name-dropping?*

*Hell-raiser Shirley MacLaine surprised outside her dressing room. "Are you Galella? You're funny!" she exclaimed.*

*Hi! I'm Bette Midler. Ya gonna love me! Wanna bet?*

*Sing a little.*

*Unzip a little.*

*Unzip a little more.*

*Hey, this is gettin' serious, folks.*

*Did I promise you Miss America?*

*Too late to stop now.*

*What the hell—they're gonna love me!*

*Well, at least I can* sing, *can't I?*

*Gloria Vanderbilt in the lobby of Avery Fisher Hall in New York.*

I've never seen famed Surrealist Salvador Dali without that black velvet jacket and the fancy walking stick. As for his companions here at the St. Regis—Guy Burgos and model Appolonia—he runs automatically, but her you have to wind up.

Halston (the designer) and Pat Ast (the actress), Beautiful People swooning ensemble at the Coty Fashion Awards.

Cosmopolitan *editor-in-chief Helen Gurley Brown of*
Sex and the Single Girl *fame.*

*Nope, she's not Helen Gurley Brown's older sister.
She's Gloria Swanson.*

*Fred Astaire and Ginger Rogers have made millions of people happy—and when I caught them together like this I could sure see why.*

*French artist-photographer Raymundo de Larrain with the woman-they-don't-get-any-more-beautiful-than: Loretta Young.*

*Ballet director Agnes DeMille, directing.*

*Prima ballerina Margot Fonteyn looking just the way a prima ballerina is supposed to look. Bravo, Margot! (That's New York Senator Jacob Javits, who's probably whispering the same thing.)*

*Chaplin! Need I say more?*

*Charlie's daughter Geraldine. Note the resemblance in the puckish mouth.*

*Composer-conductor Leonard Bernstein at a Eugene McCarthy fund-raising dinner.*

*Conductor Leopold Stokowski at his ninetieth birthday party.*

*Ladies and gentlemen, Louis Armstrong!*

*A tough gal and a tirelessly robust performer—Eartha Kitt.*

*Composer-arranger-pianist Duke Ellington at a Rainbow Room party in his honor.*

*The king of them all! Director John Huston.*

*Candice and director Mike Nichols. He made* The Graduate *and* Who's Afraid of Virginia Woolf?

*If Candice Bergen asked me to deck those two guys, I'd do it. But I just took her picture and blew her a kiss.*

*Candice Bergen.*

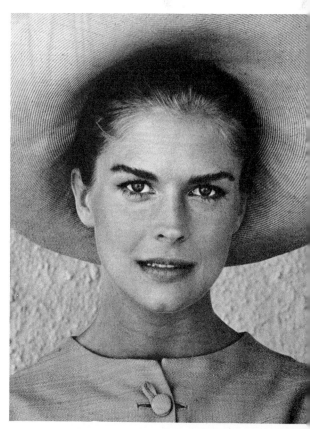

*Christie's trying to dodge the autograph hound on the left. She did. But I was too quick for her.*

*It's the hair that does it—the sort of blown look it has here. But Julie can be very soft, very winsome, as she was in Petulia. Few actresses have played as varied roles as well.*

*Warren Beatty and Julie Christie share thigh and 3-D glasses at Greenwich Village film screening.*

118

*I shot this one of Julie at Lake Geneva in Switzerland. You usually don't go for arty shots when you're a paparazzo—but I'll stack this picture up against any photo study of Julie you show me.*

*Here's Julie in a Malibu market, where I caught her shoeless looking over the luncheon meats.*

I caught Richard Harris between takes filming
Cromwell. *The guy is actually playing
football with his shoe. Yes, Virginia,
it can get mighty boring making
movies.*

*Charlton Heston.*

*Charlton Heston sketching during a break on the* Julius Caesar *set.*

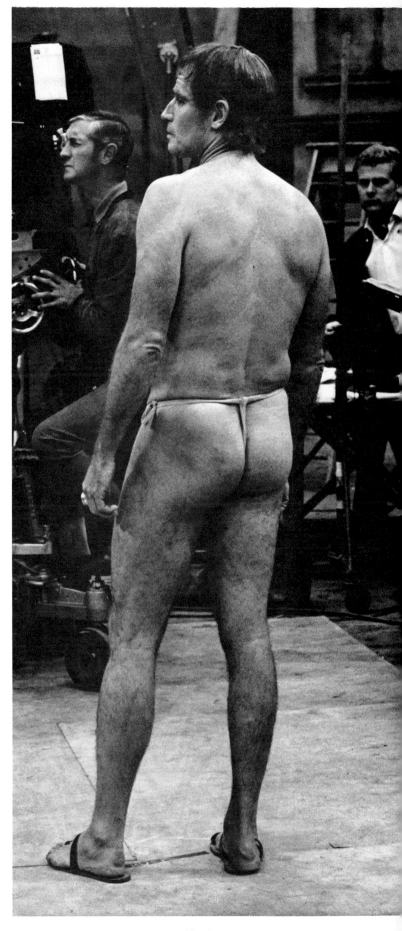

*Charlton Heston without his chariot.*

121

*Mia's got a face that could make the angels cry. I spotted her standing in front of Tiffany's.*

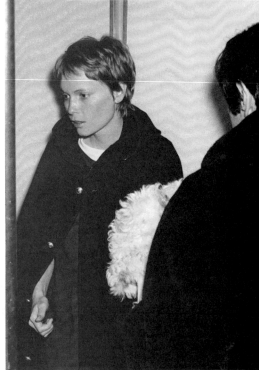

*Here's the first shot of actress Mia Farrow and composer-pianist André Previn before they got married, and I was the one to get the shot.*

*Polish film director Roman Polanski chewing on a cigar beside Sharon Tate.*

*Janet Raymond, well-known Marilyn Monroe look-alike, claims to be Marilyn's daughter.*

*You can see the snow coming down as Ari tries to get a cab and Jackie waits inside to keep out the weather and away from the paparazzi.*

*Jackie strolling toward the intersection of Madison and 88th. I shot this one from a taxi—and it will always be my favorite. It sort of says something like "See the thoroughbred striding."*

*Jackie and Ari arriving at John F. Kennedy International Airport with bodyguards and Olympic Airlines personnel trying to block my getting a picture.*

*Jackie under Secret Service escort as she leaves a private screening on 56th Street.*

# Jackie

It's tough for me to go into my feeling about Jacqueline Kennedy Onassis, what this woman continues to mean to me. The court battle she brought us both into was so widely publicized, people have probably formed all sorts of opinions about my pursuit of her. Well, I admit that much of it, yes. I *did* pursue her. And why not? Is there a more compelling woman smiling down on us from the heights of the famed? I don't think so. And I admit to being obsessed with tearing after every reasonable and fair opportunity to photograph this splendid woman—to make a lasting record of her infinite moods and endlessly varied comings and goings. There was something in me always insisting that the world should have a record of all the things she does and all the ways she is. I suppose I saw her—and still do see her—as the perfect model of wife, mother, woman—someone whose ways of being should exist as instruction to all wives, all mothers, all women. There's no denying that that's a pretty obsessive way to feel—but I don't think I'm alone in this overwhelming admiration for Jackie. All of us who lived through the tragic fortunes life dealt her and who witnessed the strength, dignity and grace with which she answered life's fortunes have come to believe that Jackie represents the highest ideals of American womanhood. And I guess this is as good a time as any to say I'm deeply sorry I ever did anything to upset that good woman. I didn't mean to. I meant only well. I just wish she would see it that way too—see that my wanting to photograph her was my way of wanting to honor her. Photography is the pencil I write with—and all I was doing was writing a long love letter to a woman who set fire to my heart.

Aristotle Onassis and daughter Christina coming out of New York's elegant "21." I took this shot shortly after the death of Ari's son.

Jackie very sweet-faced at John F. Kennedy International Airport.

Jackie at the Skorpios beachhouse heading for the shower. This is the location where the nudes were taken by the other paparazzi.

When Jackie and Ari were on Skorpios, I tried all kinds of disguises to dodge the Secret Service and Greek police. Trying for the Skorpios shots stands out as the most dangerous and costly assignment of my career as a paparazzo.

*The smile, the enthusiasm tell you Caroline is a Kennedy.*

*Caroline Kennedy at the Rainbow Room.*

*Here's Lee at Lincoln Center looking like the beautiful woman she is.*

*Jackie at the RFK tennis tourney.*

*Robert Francis Kennedy at Madison Square Garden.*

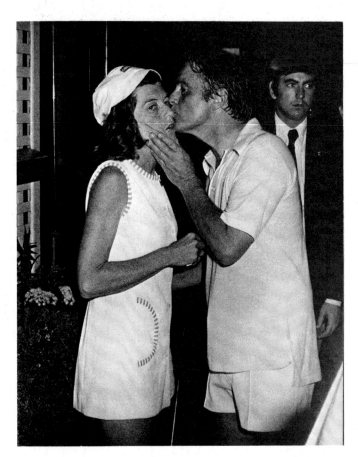

*Sargent Shriver and his wife, Eunice.*

*Eunice Shriver and Ethel Kennedy shopping along
Fifth Avenue after a skating party. That's the thing
about all the Kennedys—so much* life.

*Robert F. Kennedy, Jr. What those eyes have seen!
What that heart has heard!*

129

*Joan Kennedy.*

There is no mother who does not know what this
mother feels—and no mother who feels more than this
one does. Rose Kennedy in front of St. Francis Xavier
Church in Hyannisport.

Ethel, Teddy and Jackie at the RFK pro-celebrity
tennis tourney.

*Jackie Bouvier's sister, Lee Radziwill.*

*Rose and Ted Kennedy at a movie premiere at the Kennedy Center.*

*Ted Kennedy outside Washington hospital where his son's leg was removed owing to cancer.*

*Ethel Kennedy.*

*Ethel and Ted. The Kennedys are full of life and their spirits are vigorous.*

*Mrs. Coretta King*

*Babe Ruth's widow and the "Yankee Clipper," Joe DiMaggio. A clasping of hands that carries a weight of feeling beyond words.*

*Gregory Peck*

*Peter Sellers*

*Jimmy Stewart*

*Anthony Quinn*

*Ingrid Bergman*

*Glamorous laughter—Ingrid Bergman, Rex Harrison and Virna Lisi.*

*Ingrid Bergman, a woman capable of great feeling and no less capable of conveying a great feeling. Is there any better definition of the total woman?*

*Beauty, thy name is woman: Shakespeare. Beauty, thy name is Diahann Carroll: Galella!*

*I'm grateful Natalie Wood was easygoing enough to let me take this picture. But in that outfit she looks like "The Incredible Revenge of the Pom-Pom Girl."*

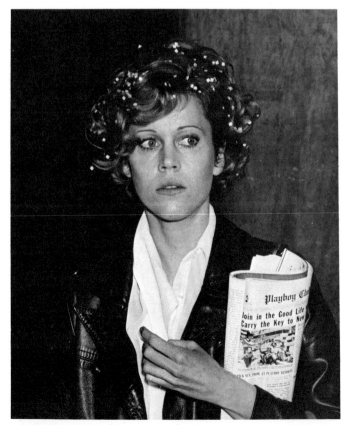

*Jane Fonda. Intelligence, depth and marvelous, soulful hands.*

*I sneaked into the Academy Awards rehearsals to catch the five Best Actress nominees looking as confused as rejects from the Ted Mack Amateur Hour: Ingrid Bergman, Natalie Wood, Jane Fonda, Diahann Carroll and Rosalind Russell.*

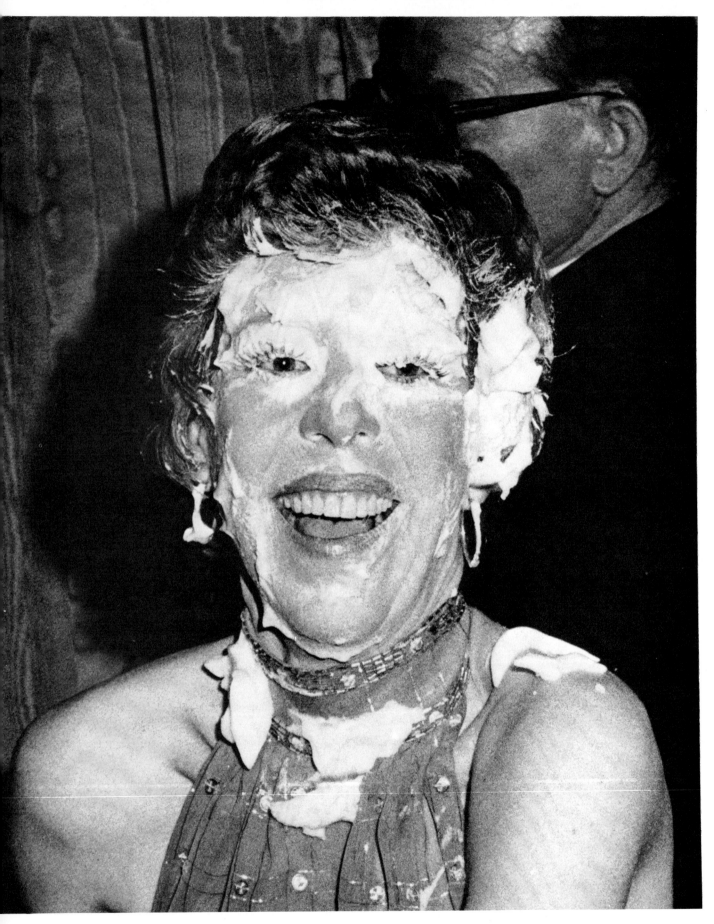

Carol Burnett: "Of course I use Gleem. Doesn't everybody?"

*Top banana Phil Silvers grabbing wife of George Bar-*
*rie (of Fabergé) and saying, "Hey, buddy, lemme show*
*you how to knot a necktie."*                    *Lucille Ball.*

This is no Benson and Hedges commercial but a legit shot of Carroll (Archie Bunker) O'Connor coming down an escalator after a party.

Hef's stuck to his pipe, I'm stuck to my camera. I always hold onto my camera with both hands—except of course when I get a chance to use one to hold onto Zoli model Angeleen.

*And you thought Dick Van Dyke was just like the boy next door! Well, he is!*

*The woman is Barbi Benton, the most famous Playmate of them all. The man is Hugh Hefner, publisher of* Playboy. *Hef's not so much famous for that as for being the first man in history to be grafted onto a pipe.*

143

*Joey Heatherton.*

*Toro or toreador? Ann-Margret and Roger Smith at the chic Jockey Club.*

*Entertainer Joey Heatherton with her bandleader dad, Ray, at the Persian Room.*

Police Woman's *Angie Dickinson and songwriter-husband Burt Bacharach.*

*Actress Sally Struthers leaving CBS studios after a night's taping of* All in the Family. *The joint's heavily guarded, so I really had to do some tiptoeing to get this one by shooting through the glass door. Looks as though Sally's doing a little tiptoeing of her own.*

*It's the light that comes from inside them that makes some of them shine around the clock. Lloyd Bridges and Dyan Cannon singing their little hearts out.*

146

*Cloris Leachman and longtime husband George Englund.*

*I got this one of Lauren at Altman's department store in New York. She looks like a pretty good Joe, you know?*

*Is she or isn't she? If you check out Lauren's eyes, you can see she expects the question.*

*Lauren with celebrated photographer Richard Avedon.*

148

*That space between her teeth is her trademark now.*
*It's what says: This is not just another pretty face.*
*Lauren Hutton.*

*Marlo Thomas at an art-gallery party. "Yes, I'm almost positive six comes after five, but if you'll just let go of my other hand we'll know for sure."*

The Beautiful People get together and sometimes look just as low-rent as you and me—for example, from left to right, Elsa Peretti, producer Jack Haley, Jr., Liza Minnelli (she's about to shake hands Hollywood-style—southpaw), fashion designer Halston and recent media-hype Margaux Hemingway.

Your basic glamorous, romantic, gilt-edged jet-setter—Marisa Berenson.

British actress Lynn Redgrave and her husband.

*I always thought director Otto Preminger was in possession of a face no less interesting than those that adorn the actors who work for him—and so I set out to prove it.*

*David Merrick and wife: Perhaps you'll like this head better.*

*Hitchcock can't help himself. He's always directing a camera. Distracted as he is here, he's probably thinking: Shoot from a little lower, Ron, so the face is more in shadow and therefore scarier.*

*The Empress and the Court Magician: Alfred Hitchcock and the ever-lovely and regal Grace Kelly at New York's Park Lane Hotel.*

*Julie Andrews in a reflective mood—caught offguard
on a movie set in Paris.*

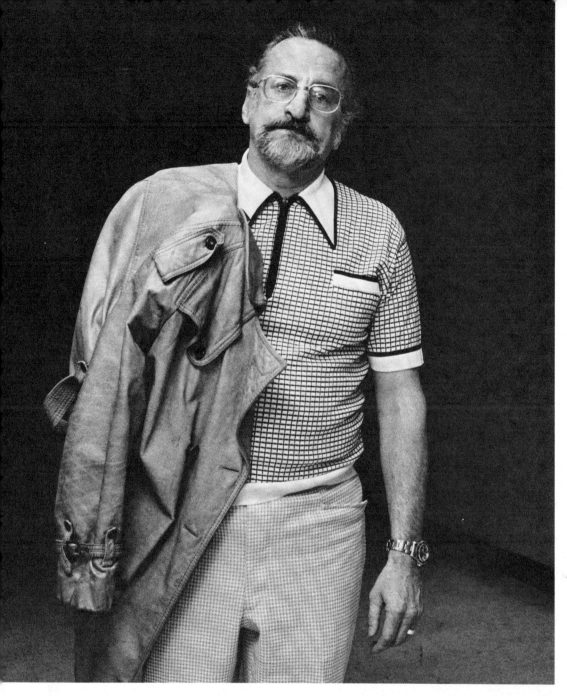

*Scott looking as if he means business (I didn't stick around to chat).*

*When somebody asks you what does a man's man mean, just show him this picture of George C. Scott.*

155

*Here's what Grant Wood's painting "American Gothic" would look like Hollywood-style: actor Robert (Marcus Welby) Young and Mrs. Young.*

*Lana Turner, looking stunned, stark and, after plenty of years, sexy enough to be discovered at Schwab's all over again.*

*Greer Garson at the* Airport *premiere. Whoever will forget her as Mrs. Miniver?*

*One of the great film-makers and actors of all time—*
*Orson Welles. Welles is what the good sultan looks*
*like in a kid's storybook. In my book, he's what a*
*good man looks like.*

157

Don Rickles: "Will the boys in the string section please *cut out the grab-ass!*"

*Angela Lansbury: If you got it, flaunt it—and if you don't got it, flaunt it anyway.*

*Burt Lancaster always puts all of his spirit into whatever he does, even if it's just the sort of chitchat that goes on at a celebrity party.*

158

*I'd leave home for Jacqueline Bisset. I'd even leave America for Jacqueline Bisset. But does she care?*

*Robert Mitchum.*

*Eternal Good Guy and Former Bad Girl—Glenn Ford and ex-pin-up Terry Moore—shown in a candid shot that, studied closely enough, could give you the fixings for a story. I've got mine—you make up yours.*

*"Excuse me," the guy on the right says, "but I couldn't help noticing how much we resemble each other, except you're a trifle taller than I am. Perhaps the carpet's thicker where you're walking?"*
*Anyway, Rock Hudson and Academy Award winner Joel Grey at the Plaza Hotel.*

With looks like this, John Lindsay
could have had a career on the screen
or the stage. Come to think of it, he
might yet.

The former Mayor of New York and
his wife, Mary. This is what people
mean when they talk about the
American Character.

162

*Two mayors, two styles, but both stylish guys. Big John Lindsay and big Abe Beame.*

*George Wallace at the Waldorf-Astoria.*

*Ex-performer and current America-firster Martha Raye with ex-performer and current politician Ronald Reagan. "All right, Corporal Raye, in the morning you're going to land on the beach and wipe out those enemy machine-gun installations. I'd love to join you in the glorious assault, but since I'm the brains in this outfit, it's my job to stay here on the ship and observe."*

*I tried for Nixon after he quit—on a special assignment from the* National Enquirer. *I camped on the San Clemente beach for one solid week, sent messages to the ex-President, pulled every trick in the world and got a great suntan but no Nixon. Meanwhile, I hung around with a 1000-mm. lens on my camera, just waiting. It was worth it. I got this shot of the former First Lady, the face of anguish.*

*You* figure it out! *I mean, if all you could know about the man is what you could tell from this picture, what would you say you see there? Pride? Arrogance? Uncertainty? Fear?*

*Before her world fell apart.*

*Henry Kissinger and wife Nancy.*

*Nancy: Don't look now, but is that Gregory Peck
sitting over there?*
*Henry: It possibly is Gregory Peck and it possibly is
not Gregory Peck. I believe there is every reason to
think that it might or might not be Gregory Peck.*

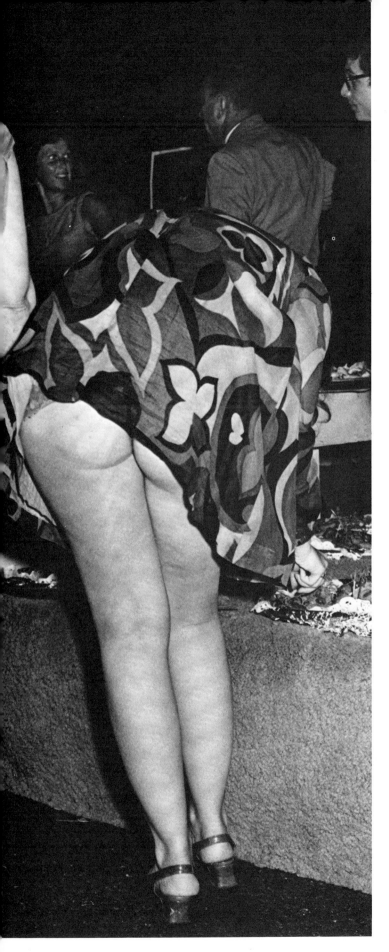

*Gerald Ford.*

*Nelson Rockefeller.*

*American Scandinavians for Rockefeller benefit at the Cheetah, New York.*

*Howard Hughes (or look-alike) and friend (and friend?).*

*Jimmy Hoffa.*

*"I'll take notes later," says columnist Earl Wilson.*

*Screen artists Liv Ullmann and Sir John Gielgud photographed at Sardi's.*

*The Duke and Duchess of Windsor at the Museum of Modern Art in New York. Do they write love stories like this anymore?*

*Clint Eastwood at Pebble Beach.*

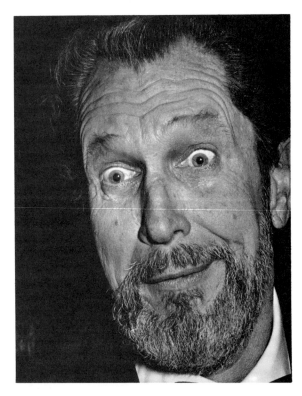

*Vincent Price.*

*Elliott Gould surprised here at New York's famous
Katz's Delicatessen. "Hey, podner, mind pointing that
salami the other way? It could be loaded, you know."*

*Dustin in Central Park helping a stray dog get a drink.*

*There's probably no actor who more forcefully expresses the New York school of acting. Pacino and De Niro are great, but Dustin started the whole thing.*

*Dustin and his wife Anne at a dinner party. Only Dustin can peer like that. You just don't know if he's laughing or burning.*

# Dustin Hoffman

If Frank Sinatra dusts off the dream of the street kid made good, Dustin Hoffman screws down the image of the street kid *still* a street kid. And I think that's the magic of Dustin's charm, the reason for his growing geography among the all-time greats. Like John Garfield before him, Hoffman doesn't seem to have been changed by stardom; like John Garfield, Hoffman gives you the feeling of a guy who couldn't change if they broke his arm to help him along—and we can sense this in the way he appears on screen, we can sense this real and unalterable quality in Hoffman's bearing. Hoffman gives you the notion of a fella just doing his work—and it just so happens his work is acting up there on the big screen.

You could add Robert Mitchum and Lee Marvin to the Garfield–Hoffman tradition, stars who convince us that they're *just like us*–meaning, just the way we think we *would* be if we were movie stars: unchanged, unchangeable, natural, unaffected by the glitter, still wise-cracking guys, still regular guys, still like the guys back on the block, only better. And richer. But judging from my experiences in shooting Dustin, I've got to be fair, because Dustin makes you want to be *double* fair. The guy really is the way you'd guess—just his old sweet self, cute as a button on a baby's nightie. And if Dustin's faking it—well, I don't think anybody's ever going to catch him at it.

The Pennsylvania coal dust got into this man and no amount of Hollywood makeup will ever cover it all over—thank God. Charles Bronson.

The big fights are a paparazzo's dream. I got Telly Savalas at the Frazier–Quarry match. Telly looks right at home.

*Mary Tyler Moore and husband, Grant Tinker.*

*Everybody's sweetheart, Mary Tyler Moore. (Can you blame them?)*

*I can't remember whether she had her hand up like that to say hi or to smack me off. You can't tell from her smile because Mary Tyler Moore is always smiling.*

*Comedian Marty Allen: "Wrap 'em to go."*

Lucille Ball: "Ricky!"

Goldie Hawn.

*Jimmy Durante: "Good night, Mrs. Calabash!"*

*Groucho Marx: "Say the secret word."*

*"You say you'll make me a star?!"* Huntington Hartford *with* Penthouse *model.*

181

*Cybill Shepherd.*

*Cicely Tyson.*

*Sidney Poitier.*

*All you have to do is look to know this is a woman who could turn you inside out and you'd come back to ask her to do it again.*

*Cher—breaking all the rules. Greg Allman helping her do it.*

184

# Cher

Cher is clearly a phenomenon of this decade, a celebrity whose fame could only have reached such heights in the aimless, somewhat mad Seventies. The Sixties were a time of revolt, of change, of loud debate and crazy enthusiasms. And it was in the Sixties that the *team* of Sonny and Cher, their *sound*, first achieved popularity. But the confused, bored Seventies gives us Cher as a single, as a style, as a personality miles distant from anything she does as a stylist of song. It is what Cher idealizes in her person that I think now seizes the imagination of millions—a steamy sexuality blatantly announced, an I-don't-give-a-damn attitude about her admirers *and* herself, a suggestion that she is about to do something really outrageous, wildly scandalous, unspeakably shocking. And every now and then she does just that—and it proves just enough to raise her enormous popularity to an even greater peak. Her break with Sonny Bono was scandalous yet expectable—just as her break with Greg Allman was scandalous yet expectable. And all of it was thrilling—because all of it was secretly our plan, too. (Who, after all, could stomach that silly clown forever—and the other one, the drawling sleepyhead with the wispy yellow hair, the one we were making plans to dump the minute we caught his act). So what it all comes down to is *anticipated* surprise— the surprise we just knew Cher was going to give us. So what's *next*, Cher? It's this question, this anticipation of something utterly provocative, that keeps us fascinated by Cher, with Cher.

*Cher in New York—looking as though she could eat you up alive.*

*I guess she just washed her hands and can't do a thing with them.*

*Yes, Virginia, this is Sonny and Cher before they were Sonny! and Cher!*

Sonny Bono with a Band-aid on his nose making a call in the foyer of CBS's Hollywood studios. I shot this photo through the glass door since no photographers are allowed in CBS studios.

Cher at New York's Metropolitan Museum of Art—an exhibit in her own right.

*Sly Stone and his ex-wife at their Madison Square Garden wedding.*

British actress Glenda Jackson: "Next time I ask for mouthwash, don't pass the Listerine, okay?"

Buddy Hackett: "If you think I look stupid, wait till you see me with a glass of Scotch on my head."

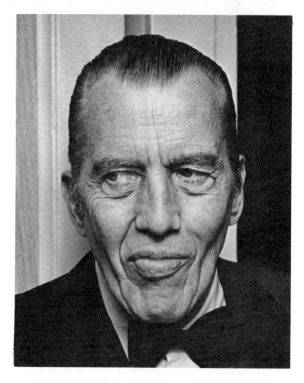

Ed Sullivan: People used to say he looked a little like Humphrey Bogart. But we'll always remember him as Mr. Show Business.

*Wilhelmina models Hanny and Kathleen Milcarek:*
*"No pictures! Well, maybe."*